Nature's Children

JACKALS

John Woodward

GROLIER

FACTS IN BRIEF

Classification of Jackals

Class: *Mammalia* (mammals)

Order: *Carnivora* (carnivores: meat-eating mammals)

Family: *Canidae* (dogs)

Genus: *Canis*

Species: Golden jackal (*Canis aureus*), side-striped (*Canis adustus*), black-backed (*Canis mesomelas*).

World distribution.   The golden jackal lives in northern and eastern Africa, the Middle East, southeast Europe, and southern Asia. The black-backed jackal lives in eastern and southern Africa. The side-striped jackal lives in central Africa.

Habitat.   From dry grasslands to damp woodlands.

Distinctive physical characteristics.   Slender, medium-sized, wolflike wild dogs with long legs and bushy tails.

Habits.   Live and hunt in families at night, dawn, and dusk.

Diet.   Mainly animals from insects to small antelopes, plus carrion from large dead animals. Also some fruit.

© 2004 The Brown Reference Group plc
Printed and bound in U.S.A.
Edited by John Farndon and Angela Koo

Published by:

An imprint of Scholastic
Library Publishing
Old Sherman Turnpike, Danbury,
Connecticut 06816

Library of Congress Cataloging-in-Publication Data
Woodward, John, 1954–
  Jackals / John Woodward.
    p. cm. — (Nature's children)
  Includes index.
  Summary: Describes the physical characteristics, habits, and natural environment of jackals.
  ISBN 0–7172–5957–9 (set)   ISBN 0–7172–5967–6
  1. Jackals—Juvenile literature. [1. Jackals.] I. Title. II. Series.

QL737.C2W67 2004
599.77'2—dc22

                       2003049173

Contents

Check any picture of lions eating their prey on an African wildlife reserve, and you will likely spot a jackal. It's the lean, foxy-looking dog trying to snatch a mouthful of meat when the lions are not looking. It looks tiny next to a lion, and it certainly has to wait its turn. A single jackal has trouble scaring off a vulture.

Yet despite this, jackals are extremely successful. They will eat almost anything and live almost anywhere. They are clever enough to find ways of dealing with foods that they have never tried before. They have a well-organized family life in which grown-up jackals help their parents look after their new litters of pups. And they have the vital ability to live alongside people. In a world where many big hunters are becoming rare, the jackals are survivors.

Opposite page:
A jackal looks a little like a pet Alsatian dog, but it is much smaller and more delicate. It stands only 14 inches (38 centimeters) high at the shoulder.

What Is a Jackal?

A jackal looks like an overgrown fox. When it is hunting mice, it even behaves like a fox, stalking and pouncing with a quick, deadly leap. But jackals are really more like small wolves. They can be very sociable and sometimes hunt together. They live in wolflike family groups, or packs. And when they bring food back to the den, they often carry it in their stomachs, just like wolves.

These differences show that jackals are more closely related to wolves than foxes. Even the first part of their scientific name, *Canis*, is the same as that of the gray wolf (*Canis lupus*). But studies of their DNA (chemical makeup) show that the three types of jackal are not particularly closely related to each other. They are just smallish, wolflike dogs that share the same name: jackal.

Long History

Scientists think that jackals are very like the dogs that lived about six million years ago. At this time a change in climate produced less rain, and grasslands started growing in place of forests. Big, fast-running animals like antelopes and gazelles started living on the grassy plains. Early foxlike dogs moved out of the forests to hunt them. To have any chance of catching their prey, the dogs had to move fast too. So, over a long period of time they developed into long-legged, tireless runners.

Some dogs have carried this to extremes. The painted hunting dogs of Africa are extremely lean and leggy, and they are specialists in hunting big animals. But the jackals have stuck with the rather foxy yet long-legged body form of their ancestors. That allows them to hunt a much wider variety of prey.

Opposite page: *Painted hunting dogs—also known as African wild dogs—are perfectly built for chasing prey. Like greyhounds, they have light bodies and long legs.*

9

Gold, Silver, and Striped

Opposite page:
Sometimes jackals, like this side-striped jackal, fight with vultures to get a bite of a zebra carcass.

There are three different types, or species, of jackal. The most widespread is the golden jackal. It lives in southern Asia, Arabia, and southeast Europe as well as northern parts of Africa. Its coat varies from golden-yellow to silver-gray, depending on the season and where it lives. Golden jackals that live in the colder parts of Asia also have much thicker coats than their African relatives.

In eastern Africa golden jackals live alongside the black-backed jackal. The black-backed jackal has a tan coat with dark fur on its back and tail. Its dark fur is mixed with silver, so it is sometimes called the silver-backed jackal. It also lives in southern Africa in a quite separate region.

The third species is the side-striped jackal, which is fawn and gray with a white streak on each flank. It lives in African woodlands, except in the far south.

The Simien Jackal

There is another animal called a jackal, but it is not really a jackal at all. The Simien jackal lives in the highlands of Ethiopia in northern Africa, in cold regions more than 10,000 feet (3,000 meters) above sea level. About 15,000 years ago the world was much colder, and there were cold regions all over Africa. Africa is now much warmer, and only a few high mountain ranges are cool enough for the Simien jackal. So the Simien jackal is now very rare, with maybe only 500 adults left.

The Simien jackal preys on small animals such as rats, using the same hunting techniques as foxes. Because of this it is sometimes known as the Simien fox instead. But scientists now believe it is a close relative of the gray wolf and coyote, so they prefer yet another name—the Ethiopian, or Abyssinian, wolf. So altogether, it's the Simien-Ethiopian-Abyssinian-jackal-fox-wolf!

Opposite page: *Simien jackals eat mole rats. Since mole rats live under the ground, the jackal sits patiently waiting for them to come up to forage.*

Size and Shape

All jackals are lightweights compared to wolves. A gray wolf can weigh anything up to 165 pounds (75 kilograms): That is as much as a grown man. But a jackal rarely weighs more than 33 pounds (15 kilograms). That's less than a big coyote, but maybe three times as much as a red fox.

So jackals are not powerful hunters like wolves. They are slim, agile animals that can survive on a diet of small animals and scraps. They are famous for the way they run rings around big, lumbering hyenas, darting in to steal food from under their noses. They are fast enough to hunt gazelles if they want. Yet they are small enough to stay out of trouble in areas where bigger hunters have been wiped out. It is a very successful combination.

Built for the Chase

The long, slim legs of a jackal show that it is built for running. It stands and runs on its toes, which have stout, blunt claws for grip. The lower bones of its front legs are locked together, so it cannot twist its front paws as we twist our hands. That makes its legs less flexible but much stronger. The jackal's backbone is also quite rigid. That gives its running muscles something solid to pull against as the jackal bounds along.

It has a deep chest with big lungs, so it can pump plenty of oxygen into its body. The oxygen helps break down blood sugar to release energy. The more oxygen it can take in with each breath, the farther it can run before it gets tired. That's called stamina, and a jackal has lots of it. It can go on chasing for hours.

Multipurpose Teeth

Like all dogs, jackals eat meat. They have extralong, sharp teeth just behind their front teeth for seizing and ripping into their prey. Many animals, including us humans, have these teeth. They are called dog teeth, or canines, because they are especially long in dogs. Farther back, in their cheeks jackals also have special bladelike teeth called carnassials. They work together to slice through tough, raw meat like scissors. All dogs, cats, hyenas, and mammal carnivores have these teeth.

But a jackal eats other things as well as meat, and they often need more chewing. So it also has chewing teeth rather like ours right at the back of its mouth. Like all dogs, jackals have long muzzles compared to cats. Cats are lone hunters and need short, strong jaws to bring down prey by themselves. Jackals hunt in packs and worry their prey. With their long jaws they can rip into their prey again and again until it drops exhausted.

Opposite page: Like all dogs, jackals have long mouths full of teeth for all purposes. Their sharp front teeth bite prey, and their scissorlike back teeth chew food.

Super Senses

As well as providing room for all its teeth, the long muzzle of a jackal has another advantage. It makes its nose very long too, so there is room for an extrabig scent-detecting system. That gives the jackal a supersensitivity to all kinds of scents. It can even track down a meal in total darkness. Most pet dogs have the same skill; and if you own a dog, you'll know all about it.

Scent isn't everything, though. A jackal has very sensitive ears, which it turns to pinpoint prey in the same way as a cat listens for the rustle of a mouse. It also has excellent eyesight and takes a keen interest in everything around it. By watching other animals, it can often discover where to find a free meal and avoid the trouble of hunting altogether. Jackals can see especially well in the dark.

Where Do Jackals Live?

Jackals live in all kinds of wooded and grassy landscapes. In eastern Africa all three species are close neighbors, but they mostly favor slightly different habitats. The black-backed jackal seems most comfortable on the dry grassland and acacia scrub of the African savannas. Here it lives alongside lions, cheetahs, spotted hyenas, and great herds of antelopes and gazelles.

Golden jackals live here too, but they can survive longer without water than the other jackals. So golden jackals range farther into drier areas, such as the deserts of the Sahara and Arabia to the north. Golden jackals are very adaptable. In Asia—where there are no other jackals—they may live almost anywhere from forests to the outskirts of towns.

Side-striped jackals avoid dry places and prefer damp woodland near rivers. That means they are quite scarce on the open plains and well outnumbered by the other two.

Opposite page: *Black-backed jackals live on African grassland called savanna. They live alongside all kinds of spectacular large creatures like this giraffe.*

What Do Jackals Eat?

You might expect a jackal to eat just meat, but it actually eats almost anything. The only common foods that it ignores are leaves and grass, which it cannot digest. But it is happy to eat all kinds of fruit, nuts, insects, worms, eggs, birds, lizards, rats, and mice. It also sometimes hunts and kills larger animals like young antelopes called gazelles.

A jackal will try anything once and is always on the lookout for an easy meal. There is no chance of a jackal going hungry because its favorite food is off the menu. It simply tries something else. So it can live in places where the food supply changes dramatically with the seasons or in deserts where food of any kind is scarce.

This jackal is chewing on a leg taken from a carcass.
But jackals eat insects and plants more often than meat.

Hunting

If a jackal is an expert at anything, it's hunting small animals such as rats. Ears pricked to catch every rustle and squeak, it creeps through the grass. It then leaps in the air to pounce straight down, pinning its victim to the ground. While the rat is still dazed, the jackal grabs it in its jaws and breaks its neck with a quick shake. One gulp and the rat is gone.

Jackals hunt small prey like this alone. But sometimes they join forces with other jackals to catch bigger victims. They often hunt in pairs for young gazelles. One jackal distracts the mother, while the other grabs her baby. Black-backed jackals may even hunt adult gazelles in packs of four or five like miniature wolves, working together to outmaneuver their victims and bring them down.

Black-backed jackals often pair up to go hunting young gazelles. One jackal lures the mother away, while the other attacks the baby gazelle.

Scavenging

Jackals have a bad name for eating carrion, the remains of dead animals. In fact, only a tenth of their food is carrion. But jackals take food wherever they find it. They often watch vultures circling in the sky to lead them to a free meal of carrion.

But when they get to the scene, they may find that lions or hyenas have got there first—or even made the kill in the first place. So they have to wait. They often get impatient, and pairs of jackals sometimes steal food from spotted hyenas. One dives in, and while the hyena chases it off, the other grabs the meat. It's a bold tactic, because a hyena could kill a jackal with a single bite.

The remains of a large dead animal may be tempting for a jackal. But to get a bite, it might have to fight off vultures and even hyenas.

Male and female jackals pair up to start a family. The couple is usually very affectionate, like these two.

Jackal Families

Sometimes jackals gather in big groups of up to 30 to feed on large dead animals. Mostly, however, they live in families. Each family is centered around a mom and a pop. With them are often a few of their grown-up pups. These young adults do not have pups of their own. If they want to breed, they must go off on their own. Meanwhile, they help look after their younger brothers and sisters, bringing food and defending them from danger.

The older members of the family look after each other, so leaving the family is a big step. But black-backed jackals eventually drive their grown-up young away. Living alone is dangerous, so black-backs from different families sometimes join up in wandering groups before forming families of their own.

Knowing Who's Boss

Opposite page: *Checking each other's fur for ticks and fleas is an important part of jackal family life. This behavior helps cement bonds between each dog.*

The adults in a jackal family all look much the same, but there is a definite pecking order. At the top are mom and pop. When the family meets up after an outing, the younger adults are careful to treat their parents with respect. They approach them with their tails between their legs or wagging slightly, crouching and often whining like pups. Sometimes, they even pretend to beg for food, just as they did when they were very small.

As long as the younger jackals show that they know who's in charge, all is well. The parents share food with them, rest close by, and even groom their fur. This is a useful way of destroying, ticks, fleas, and other bloodsuckers. It also helps the jackals learn how to communicate and stay friends.

Home Territory

Jackal pairs mark their territory with scent in exactly the same way as domestic dogs. There are no lampposts where jackals live; but if there were, the jackals would urinate against them. Instead, they scent-mark tufts of grass, rocks, bushes, and other prominent objects, especially along the territorial boundaries. Here the marks act like a smelly, invisible fence. Golden jackals also howl together to let neighbors know they are there.

If a jackal does cross into a neighbor's patch, it is usually uneasy because of the unfamiliar smell. So scaring it off is no problem. But if the neighbor is old or weak, the trespasser may stand its ground and fight. Sometimes the residents are so badly injured that they die. Then the new owners move in and take over their territory.

Opposite page:
When a stranger strays into a jackal family's patch, there may be trouble. Fights are fierce, and the fighters may be badly injured or even killed.

Helpless Pups

Opposite page:
For the first month of their lives young jackals live on their mother's milk, sucking at the teats on her belly.

Unusually for mammals, jackals pair for life. Each partnership begins with a long period of dating, when the two patrol their territory and scent-mark it together. Eventually they mate and howl as a sign of their bond. The female gives birth two months later. Often the pups are born at a time when there is plenty of food available nearby. In east Africa, for example, golden jackals have pups in January and February. That is the start of the rainy season. Gazelles are calving, and the calves make easy targets for meat-eaters.

Sometimes a mom jackal may have nine pups in a litter. Usually, though, she has three or four. To keep the pups safe from predators, she gives birth in a den such as a rock crevice or a burrow made by another animal. For the first 10 days the pups are blind and helpless; they live entirely on mom's milk. Gradually, they open their eyes. After a month they start to eat meat coughed up both by their mom and dad and by their older brothers and sisters.

Home Help

A pair of jackals can rear a small family on their own, but most have help. Typically, pups stay with their parents for a while after they have grown up. Sometimes they even come home after a few weeks on their own. These "helpers" give their parents a hand in looking after the new pups.

The pups often have to be left while the parents go off to look for food. If there are no helpers, the pups must be left alone and vulnerable—or one parent must hunt alone. Helpers can babysit while the parents are hunting or even bring extra food back to the den themselves. That way the pups rarely go hungry even if food is hard to find.

Helpers look after their own younger brothers and sisters. But they may occasionally kill and eat the pups of another family.

Opposite page: Like human infants, young jackals are never left alone. If mom and dad go hunting, another adult steps in to look after the pup.

Growing Up

Opposite page:
Jackal pups grow up together, playing with their brothers and sisters—and learning to look after each other.

About two weeks after they are born, the pups start exploring outside their nursery den under the watchful eye of an adult. When a parent or helper returns with food in its stomach, the pups surround it with their tails wagging. They jump up to lick its face to make it cough up the food. Sometimes pups chase and eat large insects around the den. By the time they are about four months old, they stop drinking their mother's milk altogether.

As they grow, the pups begin to play. Often the game is to see who's boss. They work out a pecking order, and the top pup usually manages to get more food than the others. Soon they start following the adults on hunting trips and learn the boundaries of the family territory. By the time they are six months old, they can hunt for themselves. Even so, they still rely on mom and pop for some of their food for a few months more.

If a hyena comes looking for trouble, jackals join forces to drive it off, taking turns to nip its rear.

Deadly Enemies

Although they are killers themselves, jackals have many enemies. Their pups are often carried off by eagles, and the big African martial eagle can even kill a small adult jackal. On the ground the jackals' main enemies are spotted hyenas, which have huge, powerful jaws, and also leopards.

Despite this, adult jackals are fearless when defending their young. If a hyena comes nosing around the den, the adults distract it by darting in and nipping at its heels. Two jackals may team up to attack the intruder. Each one takes turns attracting its attention, while the other bites its undefended back end. The hyena usually gives up. Meanwhile, the jackals warn the pups to stay hidden with a rumbling growl or a sharp bark. If jackals get too many visits from dangerous neighbors, they eventually give up and move to another den.

Jackals and People

Opposite page:
Jackals have unfairly got a bad name nowadays. But to the ancient Egyptians they were quite special. Anubis, the Egyptian god of the dead, had a jackal's head.

Jackals have a bad reputation. Even the word "jackal" suggests someone mean and cowardly. That is probably because of the way they are often pictured tearing at carcasses along with vultures and hyenas. They also have a taste for foods that we think are disgusting. Jackals often scavenge scraps from garbage dumps. In India golden jackals eat half-burned remains of human bodies washed up on the banks of the Ganges River. In Egypt, too, they have such a strong connection with death that the ancient Egyptian god of the dead, Anubis, had a jackal's head.

Yet jackals do a useful job cleaning up garbage and animal carrion. They also hunt the rodents that often feed on farmers' crops. And they rely on hunting far more than scavenging, so their public image is all wrong. It is even likely that many of the first pet dogs were tame jackals.

Into the Future

Occasionally jackals terrorize herds of grazing animals such as sheep. Sometimes they will also raid farmers' crops, grabbing watermelons and sugarcane. That is why they are often shot as pests. You might expect them to become rare, like wolves. But jackals can also melt away into the landscape and live almost invisibly, like foxes, feeding on small animals and scraps. Many North American coyotes live like this and are doing very well. So it seems likely that the jackals will always survive.

Yet they have their problems. Jackals are badly affected by the "mad dog" disease, rabies. Many die each year, and a bad attack can wipe out a local population. They may also spread the disease to rarer animals such as painted hunting dogs, with disastrous results.

Words to Know

Blood sugar The sugar called glucose, which is made from an animal's food and carried in the blood to where it is needed.

Canine teeth The long, pointed teeth at each side of a mammal's mouth.

Carnassial teeth The bladelike "scissor teeth" that a mammal carnivore uses to slice meat.

Carnivore Any animal that eats meat, or a special type of meat-eating mammal such as a dog, cat, or weasel.

Digest The process of breaking down food in the gut to turn it into simple substances like blood sugar.

DNA The complex chemical that contains a code describing all the features of an animal's body.

Mammal A typically hairy, warm-blooded animal that produces milk to feed its young.

Oxygen The gas in air that we need to produce large amounts of energy in the body.

Prey An animal that another animal hunts for food.

Rabies A deadly disease that especially affects dogs and foxes.

Savanna Tropical grassland.

Scent-mark To mark an object with a special scent that is recognized by neighboring animals of the same type.

INDEX

Cover Photo: Still Pictures: Martin Harvey
Photo Credits: Ardea: 18, Clem Haagner 38; Bruce Coleman: HPH Photography 7; Corbis: Gianni Dagli Orti 45; NHPA: Daryl Balfour 33, 37, Nigel J. Dennis 8, Martin Harvey 12, Christophe Ratier 42, Kevin Schafer 5, Ann & Steve Toon 21; Oxford Scientific Films: Adrian Bailey 16/17, 25, Rafi Ben-Shahar 11, Berndt Fischer 30; Still Pictures: M. & C. Denis-Huot 29, Martin Harvey 22, 26, 34, Gunter Ziesler 41.